WIP It!

The Little Book of WIP Titles

Created & Designed By
TeeCee Design Studio

Working Title: _______________________________

Genre: _______________________________

Quick Plot Line: _______________________________

____

____

____

Notes

Working Title:

Genre:

Quick Plot Line:

Notes

Working Title:

Genre:

Quick Plot Line:

Notes

Working Title: __________________________

Genre: __________________________

Quick Plot Line: __________________________

Notes

Working Title: _______________________

Genre: _______________________

Quick Plot Line: _______________________

____

____

____

Notes

Working Title: ________________________________

Genre: ________________________________

Quick Plot Line: ______________________________
____
____
____

Notes

Working Title: ___________________________

Genre: ___________________________

Quick Plot Line: ___________________________

____

____

____

Notes

Working Title: ______________________________

Genre: ______________________________

Quick Plot Line: ______________________________

Notes

Working Title: ______________________________

Genre: ______________________________

Quick Plot Line: ______________________________

____

____

____

Notes

Working Title:

Genre:

Quick Plot Line:

Notes

Working Title:

Genre:

Quick Plot Line:

Notes

Working Title: ______________________

Genre: ______________________

Quick Plot Line: ______________________

____

____

____

Notes

Working Title:

Genre:

Quick Plot Line:

Notes

Working Title:

Genre:

Quick Plot Line:

Notes

Working Title:

Genre:

Quick Plot Line:

Notes

Working Title: _______________________________

Genre: _______________________________

Quick Plot Line: _______________________________

____

____

____

Notes

Working Title:

Genre:

Quick Plot Line:

Notes

Working Title: ______________________________

Genre: ______________________________

Quick Plot Line: ______________________________

____

____

____

Notes

Working Title:

Genre:

Quick Plot Line:

Notes

Working Title: _______________________________

Genre: _______________________________

Quick Plot Line: _______________________________

____

____

____

Notes

Working Title:

Genre:

Quick Plot Line:

Notes

Working Title: _______________________

Genre: _______________________

Quick Plot Line: _______________________

Notes

Working Title: _______________________________

Genre: _______________________________

Quick Plot Line: _______________________________

____

____

____

Notes

Working Title:

Genre:

Quick Plot Line:

Notes

Working Title:

Genre:

Quick Plot Line:

Notes

Working Title: _______________________________

Genre: _______________________________

Quick Plot Line: _______________________________

____

____

____

Notes

Working Title:

Genre:

Quick Plot Line:

Notes

Working Title:

Genre:

Quick Plot Line:

Notes

Working Title:

Genre:

Quick Plot Line:

Notes

Working Title:

Genre:

Quick Plot Line:

Notes

Working Title: ______________________

Genre: ______________________

Quick Plot Line: ______________________

____

____

____

Notes

____

____

____

____

____

____

____

____

____

____

____

____

____

____

____

____

____

Working Title: _______________________________

Genre: _______________________________

Quick Plot Line: _______________________________

Notes

Working Title:

Genre:

Quick Plot Line:

Notes

Working Title:

Genre:

Quick Plot Line:

Notes

Working Title:

Genre:

Quick Plot Line:

Notes

Working Title: ___________________________

Genre: ___________________________

Quick Plot Line: ___________________________

____

____

____

Notes

Working Title:

Genre:

Quick Plot Line:

Notes

Working Title:

Genre:

Quick Plot Line:

Notes

Working Title:

Genre:

Quick Plot Line:

Notes

Working Title:

Genre:

Quick Plot Line:

Notes

Working Title:

Genre:

Quick Plot Line:

Notes

Working Title: ___________________________

Genre: ___________________________

Quick Plot Line: ___________________________

____

____

____

Notes

Working Title: _______________________

Genre: _______________________

Quick Plot Line: _______________________

____

____

____

Notes

Working Title:

Genre:

Quick Plot Line:

Notes

Working Title:

Genre:

Quick Plot Line:

Notes

Working Title: ______________________________

Genre: ______________________________

Quick Plot Line: ____________________________
____
____
____

Notes

Working Title: ______________________________

Genre: ______________________________

Quick Plot Line: ______________________________

____

____

____

Notes

Working Title: ______________________

Genre: ______________________

Quick Plot Line: ______________________

____

____

____

Notes

Working Title: _______________________

Genre: _______________________

Quick Plot Line: _______________________

____

____

____

Notes

Working Title: ___________________________

Genre: ___________________________

Quick Plot Line: _____________________

Notes

Working Title: _______________________

Genre: _______________________

Quick Plot Line: _______________________

____

____

____

Notes

Working Title:

Genre:

Quick Plot Line:

Notes

Working Title: ______________________

Genre: ______________________

Quick Plot Line: ______________________

____

____

____

Notes

Working Title: ___________________________________

Genre: ___________________________________

Quick Plot Line: _________________________________

____

____

____

Notes

Working Title:

Genre:

Quick Plot Line:

Notes

Working Title:

Genre:

Quick Plot Line:

Notes

Working Title:

Genre:

Quick Plot Line:

Notes

Working Title:

Genre:

Quick Plot Line:

Notes

Working Title: ___________________________

Genre: ___________________________

Quick Plot Line: ___________________________

____

____

____

Notes

Working Title: ___________________________

Genre: ___________________________

Quick Plot Line: ___________________________

Notes

Working Title:

Genre:

Quick Plot Line:

Notes

Working Title: __________________________

Genre: __________________________

Quick Plot Line: __________________________

____

____

____

Notes

Working Title:

Genre:

Quick Plot Line:

Notes

Working Title:

Genre:

Quick Plot Line:

Notes

Working Title:

Genre:

Quick Plot Line:

Notes

Working Title:

Genre:

Quick Plot Line:

Notes

Working Title: _______________________

Genre: _______________________

Quick Plot Line: _______________________

____

____

____

Notes

Working Title: _______________________

Genre: _______________________

Quick Plot Line: _______________________

Notes

Working Title:

Genre:

Quick Plot Line:

Notes

Working Title: _______________________

Genre: _______________________

Quick Plot Line: _______________________

Notes

Working Title: ______________________________

Genre: ______________________________

Quick Plot Line: ______________________________

____

____

____

Notes

Working Title:

Genre:

Quick Plot Line:

Notes

Working Title: ___________________________

Genre: ___________________________

Quick Plot Line: ___________________________

____

____

____

Notes

Working Title:

Genre:

Quick Plot Line:

Notes

Working Title: _______________________________

Genre: _______________________________

Quick Plot Line: _______________________________

____

____

____

Notes

Working Title:

Genre:

Quick Plot Line:

Notes

Working Title:

Genre:

Quick Plot Line:

Notes

Working Title: ________________________________

Genre: ________________________________

Quick Plot Line: ________________________________

Notes

Working Title: ______________________________

Genre: ______________________________

Quick Plot Line: ______________________________

____

____

____

Notes

Working Title: ___________________________

Genre: ___________________________

Quick Plot Line: ___________________________

____

____

____

Notes

Working Title:

Genre:

Quick Plot Line:

Notes

Working Title: _______________________________

Genre: _______________________________

Quick Plot Line: _______________________________

____

____

Notes

Working Title: _______________________

Genre: _______________________

Quick Plot Line: _______________________

Notes

Working Title:

Genre:

Quick Plot Line:

Notes

Working Title:

Genre:

Quick Plot Line:

Notes

Working Title: _______________________________

Genre: _______________________________

Quick Plot Line: _______________________________

____

____

Notes

____

____

____

____

____

____

____

____

____

____

____

____

____

____

Working Title:

Genre:

Quick Plot Line:

Notes

Working Title:

Genre:

Quick Plot Line:

Notes

Working Title: ______________________

Genre: ______________________

Quick Plot Line: ______________________

____

____

____

Notes

Working Title: _______________________

Genre: _______________________

Quick Plot Line: _______________________

____

____

Notes

Working Title:

Genre:

Quick Plot Line:

Notes

Working Title: ___________________________

Genre: ___________________________

Quick Plot Line: ___________________________

____

____

____

Notes

Working Title: ______________________________

Genre: ______________________________

Quick Plot Line: ______________________________

____

____

____

Notes

Working Title:

Genre:

Quick Plot Line:

Notes

Working Title: ___________________________

Genre: ___________________________

Quick Plot Line: ___________________________

____

____

____

Notes

Working Title: _______________________

Genre: _______________________

Quick Plot Line: _______________________

____

____

____

Notes

Working Title:

Genre:

Quick Plot Line:

Notes

Working Title: _______________________________

Genre: _______________________________

Quick Plot Line: _______________________________

Notes

Working Title: _______________________

Genre: _______________________

Quick Plot Line: _______________________

____

____

____

Notes

Working Title:

Genre:

Quick Plot Line:

Notes

Thank you so much for your purchase.

I really do hope that this book has helped you,
even in some small way.

Would you like to see different designs/styles?

I am always very happy to hear from customers,
so please feel free to email me on

teeceedesignstudio@yahoo.com